PARIS

PARIS

THE CITY OF LIGHT

ALASTAIR HORNE

amber
BOOKS

Published by
Amber Books Ltd
United House
North Road
London
N7 9DP
United Kingdom
www.amberbooks.co.uk
Appstore: itunes.com/apps/amberbooksltd
Facebook: www.facebook.com/amberbooks
Twitter: @amberbooks

Project Editor: Sarah Uttridge
Designers: Zoë Mellors
Picture Research: Terry Forshaw, Justin Willsdon

ISBN: 978-1-78274-664-5

Printed in China

1 4 6 8 10 9 7 5 3 2

Contents

Introduction

P aris is always remarkable. It is, as Charles Dickens said in 1844, 'the most extraordinary place in the world'. From its foundation more than two millennia ago as a small town on the Île de la Cité, to its existence today as one of the world's most vibrant cities, Paris has retained a charm of its own, fascinating not only Dickens but also a wealth of writers, painters, soldiers and politicians. The photographs in this book will give you a sense of how the city manages to remain extraordinary not only to visiting tourists, but even to its inhabitants. Across five

chapters, we'll look not only at its magnificent sights – its buildings, museums, galleries, statues and sculptures, each with their own complex and turbulent history – but also at its everyday side: the transport networks that underpin the city, blending function with beauty as they make the city work; the shops, restaurants, cafés, offices and parks used daily by the more than two million people who live in this most beautiful of cities. We'll see Paris after dark, when the city of light brilliantly lives up to its name, and explore it in the daytime too. Magical, beautiful and frequently astonishing, it is anything but ordinary.

ABOVE:
Diners enjoy an autumn meal in one of the Place de la Sorbonne's many restaurants.

RIGHT:
Completed in 1889, the Eiffel Tower is one of Paris's most famous landmarks.

Everyday Paris

Paris may be one of the most popular tourist destinations in the world – more than 36 million holidaymakers visited the city in 2016 – but it is also home to more than two million people, plus another 4.5 million in the suburbs. For them, the sights that daily astonish and enthral visitors, from the Eiffel Tower to the Arc de Triomphe, may be just part of the furniture, unnoticed commonplace features they pass on their way to and from work each morning and evening.

And yet the beauty of the city must surely have some effect on the daily lives of its inhabitants. Even the most everyday of activities may take place in spectacular surroundings: keeping fit in the large public parks at Belleville, Buttes-Chaumont and the Bois de Boulogne, working in the remarkable hollow cube of La Grande Arche de la Défense, or shopping on the Champs-Élysées or under the immense glass canopy at the refurbished Forum des Halles, for instance. The past few decades have seen Paris renewed, with new developments across the city, such as Bercy in the east, where former wine warehouses have been converted into shops and restaurants as part of a bustling and fashionable new retail village. These striking new structures often stand side by side with reminders of the city's past, offering further evidence of the city's ability to make itself anew for each generation.

OPPOSITE:
Painter, Fontaine de Médicis, Jardin du Luxembourg
The Fontaine de Médicis has changed considerably since it was commissioned by Marie de Médici, the widow of King Henry IV, in the 1630s. The central statues of Polyphemus discovering Acis and Galatea were added in the 1860s, when the fountain was moved 30m (100ft) to make way for the rue de Médicis.

LEFT:

Approaching the Eiffel Tower, via the Champ de Mars

Once a market garden for the citizens of Paris, the Champ de Mars today offers a picturesque approach to the Eiffel Tower. However, it also has a bloody history: fifty people were killed here by soldiers in July 1791; two years later, the man held responsible for the massacre, the city's first mayor, Jean Sylvain Bailly, was guillotined here.

OPPOSITE:

Sunset at the Jardin des Tuileries

The ponds at the Jardin des Tuileries are popular meeting places. The larger of the two, the Bassin Octogonal, stands between the Musée de l'Orangerie, a gallery of impressionist and post-impressionist paintings, and the Galerie Nationale du Jeu de Paume, an arts centre for mechanical and electronic imagery from the 20th and 21st centuries.

OPPOSITE:

Carrousel de la Tour Eiffel
Around twenty carousels
can be found on the streets
of Paris, from the Carrousel
des Impressionistes on Gare
Montparnasse square to
the Carrousel de la Tour
Eiffel (pictured). The city
is also home to a dedicated
fairground museum, la Musée
des Arts Forains, which
contains one of the world's
largest private collections
of rides, attractions and
fairground art.

LEFT:

Paris in the rain
On average, it rains almost
every second day in Paris.
In 1910, however, excessive
rain during the winter led
to the flooding of the city
in late January as the Seine
rose more than 8m (26ft)
above its usual levels. Though
no deaths were reported,
the damage to the city was
considerable.

OPPOSITE:

Jogger passes Eiffel Tower

Jogging is increasingly popular in Paris. Visitors to the city can even sign up for guided running tours, and visit the sights while keeping fit. For the more serious runner, the annual Paris marathon is one of the world's largest.

RIGHT:

Ice skating in front of the Hôtel de Ville

The most popular of Paris's ice rinks each winter is at Hôtel de Ville, the city hall, though other temporary rinks are set up each year in unusual locations: on the first floor of the Eiffel Tower, for instance, and the top floor of the Montparnasse Tower, 210m (700ft) above ground!

OPPOSITE:

Covered steps at the Parc de Belleville

Built in 1988, the Parc de Belleville was created by architect François Debulois and landscaper Paul Brichet, and is the highest in Paris, at 108m (350ft). It contains more than a thousand trees and shrubs, the city's longest waterfall, at 100m (330ft), and an open-air theatre.

LEFT:

Escalator at the Pompidou Centre

The unusual design of the Pompidou Centre places all the building's infrastructure on the outside – including the escalators! They consequently offer excellent views of the area.

LEFT:

La marché aux fleurs, Île de la Cité

A daily flower market has stood at Place Louis Lépine, between Notre-Dame and Sainte-Chapelle chapel, for around 200 years; on Sundays, it is the site of the marché aux oiseaux, a market selling a wide range of birds, from chickens to macaws.

RIGHT:

The Clos Montmartre vineyard

Montmartre was once home to several vineyards owned by local churches, but these had all disappeared by 1933, when the city council approved the establishment of the Clos Montmartre vineyard on waste ground not far from the Saint-Vincent cemetery. Its annual festival, La Fête des Vendanges de Montmartre, has been known to attract more than 300,000 visitors.

Parc des Buttes-Chaumont
Opened in 1867, the Parc
des Buttes-Chaumont was
built on the site of a former
gypsum and limestone quarry.
The landscaping process took
two years to complete, but the
park now enjoys spectacular
views of the city from its
steep hills.

**Boats for hire at the
Bois de Boulogne**
Formerly a hunting ground
for France's kings, the Bois
de Boulogne was created
between 1852 and 1858 and
is now Paris's second largest
park. In 1783, the first manned
free flight took off from
the Château de la Muette,
a former hunting lodge on
the edge of the park, when
Pilâtre de Rozier and the
Marquis d'Arlandes flew to
a height of 910m (3000ft) in
a hot air balloon built by the
Montgolfier brothers.

Steps, Montmartre
Montmartre – literally,
'mount of the martyrs' –
takes its name from Saint
Denis, a Christian bishop
who was decapitated by
the Romans around 250 AD.
Statues of Saint Denis show
him carrying his severed head
in front of him.

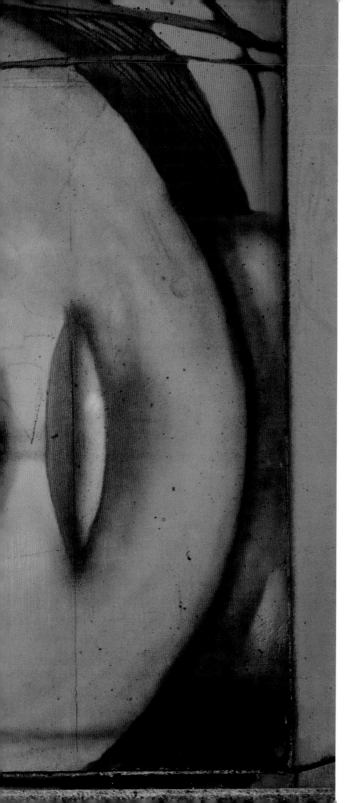

LEFT:

Mural painting at the Parc de Belleville

Parisian street artist Julien Malland, also known as Seth Globepainter, has become famous for his colourful murals of children. They have appeared not only in Paris but also in Canada, China, Chile and Indonesia.

RIGHT:

Birds fly past the funnels of the Pompidou Centre

The white funnels outside the Pompidou Centre once functioned as ventilation shafts for the building's underground areas, but are now merely decorative.

OPPOSITE:

Lunch on the steps of La Grande Arche de la Défense

Most of the 35 floors of La Grande Arche de la Défense are filled with offices; the steps at the front of the building are a popular place for workers to enjoy their lunch break.

RIGHT TOP:

La Musée des Égouts de Paris

Paris's sewers have been famous ever since Victor Hugo set some pivotal scenes from his novel *Les Misérables* within them. One of the city's more unusual museums, the Paris Sewer Museum offers a history of the city's waste disposal channels from ancient times to the present day.

RIGHT BOTTOM:

Terminal 2 at Charles de Gaulle International Airport

Opened in 1974, Charles de Gaulle International Airport serves more than 60 million passengers each year. It is named after General Charles de Gaulle, president of France for more than a decade and leader of the French resistance during World War II.

Platforms at Gare du Nord
Since 1994, Gare du Nord has been the Paris terminus for Eurostar trains from London. Up to eighteen trains run from London to Paris each day, leaving St Pancras station and arriving at Gare du Nord around two hours and fifteen minutes later. TGV and Thalys services also depart from the station, connecting the city with Brussels, Amsterdam, Dortmund and Cologne.

PREVIOUS PAGES:

**Canopy, the Forum
des Halles**
Originally opened in 1979,
the shopping centre at
the Forum des Halles was
thoroughly reconstructed
between 2010 and 2016. Its
new ceiling, the Canopy, was
designed by architects Patrick
Berger and Jacques Anziutti
and comprises 18,000 pieces
of glass.

OPPOSITE:

**Glass ceiling, Le Passage
du Grand Cerf**
Named after the wooden
stag's head that adorns one of
its shopfronts, Le Passage du
Grand Cerf is one of the most
striking of the many covered
passageways that sprung up
over Paris during the 18th and
19th centuries.

RIGHT:

**Antiquarian bookshop on
the rue Mazarine**
The streets of Paris are home
to a great many antiquarian
bookshops, particularly on
the rue de Médicis, opposite
the Jardin du Luxembourg.
Pictured is the shop of F.
Chanut on rue Mazarine, a
ten-minute walk away.

OPPOSITE:

Abercrombie & Fitch, Champs-Élysées
The American clothing chain Abercrombie & Fitch opened a 3000 sq m (31,000 sq ft) store on the historic Champs-Élysées in 2011. Frescoes inside the store show hunting scenes and athletic activities.

LEFT:

Escalators, Le Bon Marché Rive Gauche
Describing itself as 'the most selective department store in Paris', Le Bon Marché Rive Gauche was also the city's first, opening in 1852. Its founder, Aristide Boucicaut, worked with architect Louis-Charles Boileau to create the store, which inspired Émile Zola's novel *Au Bonheur des Dames* and the television series adapted from it, *The Paradise*.

ABOVE:

Stairs and escalator, Bercy
The Bercy neighbourhood has seen considerable amounts of redevelopment in recent years, including the construction of a sporting arena that will host part of the 2024 Olympic Games, and the Cour Saint-Émilion shopping complex.

BELOW:

Commuter cycles past the Arc de Triomphe

In 2015, Paris city council announced ambitious plans to turn the city into the cycling capital of the world by 2020, trebling the number of journeys made by bicycle and adding 10,000 cycle parking spaces around the city.

RIGHT:

Vélib' cycle rack

Launched in 2007, Paris's Vélib' cycle hire scheme is the world's largest outside China, with around 14,500 bicycles available at more than 1200 stations across the city – one for every hundred residents.

OPPOSITE:

Bicycle outside the Odette patisserie

Outside Odette's, one of the city's many patisseries, stands an old-fashioned bicycle adorned with flowers that match the building's décor.

OPPOSITE:
Window display, Paris boutique

For generations, Paris has been known as Europe's most fashionable city. Stores and boutiques such as Le Bon Marché, Printemps and Robert Clergerie have helped continue that reputation into the 21st century.

RIGHT:
Shop window display of colourful leather gloves

Shopping has always been a popular pastime in Paris, and in recent years new retail districts have sprung up all over the city. The recently rebuilt Forum des Halles stands on the site of an old food market.

Mannequin legs in the Printemps department store
Founded in 1865 by Jules Jaluzot and Jean-Alfred Duclos, Printemps pioneered several new practices in Parisian retail: it was the first store with electric lighting, and to have discount sales. It now also has several branches in Asia and the Middle East.

Shop window, Lancel, the Champs-Élysées
The luxury leather goods company Lancel was founded in Paris in 1876 by husband and wife Alphonse and Angèle Lancel. Originally, it sold pipes and smoking accessories, but soon switched to focus on handbags.

Model of Pinocchio at La marché aux fleurs
The daily flower market La marché aux fleurs sells not just flowers but also all sorts of garden-related accessories from its art nouveau pavilions on the Île de la Cité.

LEFT:

Librairie François Jousseaume, Galerie Vivienne
Jousseaume's Ancient and Modern bookshop was founded in 1826 and can be found in the picturesque covered passage of Galerie Vivienne, which opened the same year.

OPPOSITE:

Artists' stalls at Place du Tertre, Montmartre
Three hundred artists are permitted to sell their work at Montmartre's historic Place du Tertre. Each 1 sq m (10 sq ft) stand is shared by a pair of artists, who pay an annual fee of more than 300 Euro (£265 or $365).

LEFT:

Shakespeare and Company, rue de la Bûcherie

Taking its name from an earlier Paris bookshop frequented by modernist writers including Ezra Pound, James Joyce and Djuna Barnes, Shakespeare and Company is a popular bookshop and literary venue. Many of its staff are 'tumbleweeds', aspiring writers who sleep in the store in return for working a few hours, reading a book a day, and writing a single-page autobiography for the archives.

BELOW LEFT:

Antiques market, Marché aux Puces de Saint-Ouen

Founded in 1885, the antique and second-hand market at Saint-Ouen is the world's largest. Open only on Saturdays, Sundays and Mondays, it hosts fourteen individual markets and more than 1700 dealers, and has been a protected heritage zone since 2001.

OPPOSITE:

Patisserie and café in Paris's Jewish quarter, Le Marais

Paris's best-known Jewish neighbourhood can be found in the Marais district; it is known as the Pletzl, which means 'little place' in Yiddish. A plaque on the corner of the rue des Rosiers (pictured), explains the history of the Jewish community in the area.

LEFT:

A sunny day in Montmartre
The sidestreets of Montmartre are home to many small shops, boutiques and galleries, selling a wide range of goods including clothes, books and crafts.

ABOVE:

Passage du Chantier, rue de Faubourg Saint-Antoine
The historic cobbled Passage du Chantier, home to furniture-makers since the 15th century, offers a remarkable contrast to the busy rue de Faubourg Saint-Antoine nearby.

The river Seine
Stretching from 30km
(19 miles) northwest of Dijon,
through Paris to the English
Channel at Le Havre, the
Seine takes its name from
Sequana, the Latin name
for the goddess of the river,
worshipped by the Gauls.

**Bouquiniste stall by
the Seine**
The open-air bookstalls of
the Bouquinistes have stood
on the banks of the river
Seine since the 16th century. A
popular but apocryphal story
says that the trade began when
a boat transporting books
sank in the river near Notre-
Dame, and its sailors sold the
books they saved to passers-by.

A Taste of Paris

Parisians love their food and drink, and this chapter aims to give you a flavour of their lives. We'll explore the tastes of Paris, beginning with a view through patisserie windows and ending with absinthe, the notorious wormwood-based liqueur that reportedly drove its drinkers mad. We'll travel from bistro to brasserie, and from café to crêperie, on a gastronomic tour of the city, taking in the bustling open-air markets of Marché Barbès and Marché Président-Wilson, and the elegant art nouveau dining room of Bouillon Chartier, the cheese shops of Henri Androuet, and even a vegetarian butcher!

We'll encounter writers like Hemingway, Proust, Sartre and Marcel Aymé, artists including Picasso, Modigliani and Diego Rivera, and the rather less savoury Jean l'écorcheur, the butcher who served as an assassin for Catherine de Medici. We'll discover which foods and drinks can truly be called French, and which are perhaps less authentically French than they might at first appear. And we'll also take several steps back in time, visiting the city's oldest sweetshop and one of its earliest cafés, and finding out not only how bread proved revolutionary in the 18th century, but also what role doughnuts played in World War I.

With madeleines, oysters, salads, soups and even ice cream, there'll be something on the menu for everyone, from the sweetest tooth to the most serious gourmand. So, tuck in your napkin, raise your glass, and prepare for an absolute feast!

OPPOSITE:
Maison Lacombe, rue des Acacias
The window displays of Paris patisseries are often a work of art themselves, tempting passers-by to step inside for a cake or a pastry. Maison Lacombe, not far from the Arc de Triomphe, is no exception.

RIGHT:

Ice cream vendor smiles, despite the rain

You can buy ice cream in Paris whatever the weather! As well as the popular outdoor stands, there are many dedicated ice cream parlours in the city, from Une Glace à Paris in the Marais to Pascal le Glacier, near the Bois de Boulogne.

FAR RIGHT:

Doughnut and crêpe stand, the Bastille

Doughnuts may be most commonly associated with America, but they're an increasingly popular sight in Paris too. In 1917, during World War I, Salvation Army volunteers in France made almost 10,000 doughnuts daily for the American soldiers fighting there.

LEFT TOP:

La Rotonde, Montparnasse
One of the city's most famous brasseries, La Rotonde stands on the corner of boulevard du Montparnasse and boulevard Raspail. Opened in 1911 by Victor Libion, it was frequented in its early years by artists including Picasso, Modigliani and Diego Rivera.

LEFT BOTTOM:

Eating outside at a Paris bistro
Paris's bistros have been popular places to eat and drink for generations, but in the 1990s they were shaken up by a new movement that became known as 'Bistronomie'. Just as the name combines the fine dining of gastronomy with the unpretentious location of the bistro, so the movement focuses on offering high-quality cuisine in informal settings, at affordable prices.

OPPOSITE:

Café, Le Marais
The formerly aristocratic district of the Marais became the bohemian quarter after the French Revolution. Alongside its many museums, it is now also home to a great many cafés and bars.

LEFT:

Le Café Montmartre

On the corner of rue Norvins and rue Jean-Baptiste-Clément, the Café Montmartre stands halfway between Sacré-Cœur and the Place Marcel Aymé, named after the famous Parisian writer who situated many of his best-known works in the neighbourhood.

RIGHT:

Le Bizuth, Boulevard Saint Germain

The Boulevard Saint Germain has been famous for its cafés and nightlife since the 1930s, when writers such as Jean-Paul Sartre and Simone de Beauvoir passed their time at café≠s like Les Deux Magots, a few minutes' walk from Le Bizuth (pictured).

OPPOSITE:
La Chaise au Plafond, Le Marais
Xavier Denamur's popular brasserie La Chaise au Plafond
stands near the intersection of the leafy sidestreet of the rue de
Trésor and the bustling rue Vieille du Temple, at the heart of the
Marais district.

ABOVE:
Crêpe from a Paris street vendor
Stands selling sweet crêpes and savoury galettes are a regular
sight on the streets of Paris, particularly around Notre-Dame on
the Île de la Cité. You can watch your crêpe as it cooks on the
hotplate before being folded into a triangle for you to eat.

LEFT:
Au Lys d'Argent Crêperie, rue Saint-Louis en l'Île
The crêperie Au Lys d'Argent ('At the Silver Lily') is one of the
many restaurants to be found on the busy rue Saint-Louis en
l'Île, on Paris's historic Île Saint-Louis. In addition to crêpes,
it also offers a range of meals including salads, soups and
ice cream.

PREVIOUS PAGES:
Man entering grocery store
Many of Paris's small
independent grocery stores
display fresh produce outside,
with packaged goods inside.

LEFT:
**Oil, vinegar and bread
on display**
Hand-labelled bottles and
slices of bread stand alongside
more familiar brands in this
Paris shop display.

OPPOSITE:
Androuet, rue Mouffetard
Described by Ernest
Hemingway in *A Moveable
Feast* as a 'wonderful, narrow
crowded market street', rue
Mouffetard is one of Paris's
most prestigious market
streets. It is home to one of
the Androuet cheese shops
(pictured left); founded in
1909 by master cheesemaker
Henri Androuet, the company
now has shops in Britain and
Sweden as well as in France,
and sells more than two
hundred varieties of cheese.

Barbès Market on the boulevard de la Chapelle
Situated beneath the overhead section of Metro Line 2 on the boulevard de la Chapelle, not far from the Barbès-Rochechouart station, the Barbès Market is a bustling, cosmopolitan, open-air food market open on Wednesday and Saturday mornings.

ABOVE:

Café interior

There have been cafés in Paris since coffee was introduced to the city in the 17th century. They have remained an integral part of the city's culture ever since, providing a location not only for gossip, but also for philosophical and political debate.

RIGHT:

Café scene

Though the recent smoking ban has created challenges for Paris's café culture, it has proved resilient, and cafés remain popular places for sitting and chatting over a coffee or glass of wine.

Bouillon Chartier
Founded by brothers Frédéric and Camille Chartier in 1896, the Bouillon Chartier claims to have served fifty million meals over its 120-year history. Its dining room (pictured) has been listed as a historic site since 1989.

LEFT:

A waiter displays a selection of desserts

The sheer range of desserts available in Paris could fill a book of its own. Several have indeed appeared in works of literature, most notably Proust's famous madeleines, whose smell and taste evoke memories from the narrator's past in *À La Recherche du Temps Perdu*.

RIGHT TOP:

Waiter lights candles at Le Grand Véfour

Opened as a café in the pavilions of the Palais Royal in 1784 by Antoine Aubertot, the restaurant Le Grand Véfour spent most of the first half of the 20th century first as a low-class café and then as a venue for chess players, before reopening its doors as a restaurant in 1948.

RIGHT BOTTOM:

Café Marly

From its location in the arched terraces beneath the arcades at the Louvre, the Café Marly offers an excellent view not only of the museum's glass pyramids, but also of the celebrities who sometimes dine there.

RIGHT:

Rum Baba ready to be served, Bistrot Paul Bert

Located on the rue Paul Bert in the 11th arrondissement, the Bistrot Paul Bert is one of three restaurants founded by Bertrand Auboyneau, who in 2011 published his own book of bistro recipes with co-author and critic François Simon.

OPPOSITE TOP LEFT:

Filling glasses in a Paris restaurant

Parisian bars serve a wide range of wines, beers and spirits. In 2009, the minimum age for buying alcohol in France was raised from 16 to 18. Bars and restaurants that break this law are liable to be fined up to 7500 Euros.

ABOVE:

Baker making bread in a boulangerie in Saint-Germain-des-Prés

Bread has played a significant part at various points in French history. More than once in the 18th century, poor harvests resulted in the price of bread rising to unaffordable levels for unskilled workers, causing considerable unrest and leading to riots.

LEFT:

Fruit flan in the window of the Paul boulangerie and patisserie

Located on the prestigious Champs-Élysées, midway between the Arc de Triomphe and the Jardin de la Nouvelle France, the Paul boulangerie and patisserie is ideally placed for anyone taking a break from their shopping.

LEFT:

Baguettes in paper bags
From the long, thin, crusty loaf that we know as the archetypally French baguette, to the round pain boule and brioche, made with eggs and butter, Paris has a type of bread to suit everyone's taste.

OPPOSITE:

Parisian pastries
The range of pastries available in Paris is even wider than the range of breads. The croissant, the pain au chocolat, the éclair and the mille-feuille (literally, 'a thousand sheets') are just four delicious items that you'll find in a typical patisserie.

Brioche

CANGLÉS
$ 1.60

CROISSANT
$ AUX
1.95 NOIX

ABOVE:

Patisserie window

In France, as in Belgium, only bakeries that employ a licensed maître pâtissier ('master pastry chef') are permitted to use the title 'patisserie'. Celebrity chef Michel Roux Jnr started his career as an apprentice at the patisserie Maître Patissier, Hellegouarche, in Paris.

RIGHT:

Coffee and croissant

Coffee has been popular in Paris ever since the Café de Procope, one of the city's first coffeehouses, opened in 1686; it remains open today. By 1700, around 300 cafés were to be found across the city; by the end of the century, the number was closer to 2000.

OPPOSITE:

Croissants take pride of place in a patisserie window

Though the croissant is often seen as characteristically French, it is said to have been inspired by the kipfel, a crescent-shaped Austrian brioche reportedly created to celebrate the defeat of the Turkish army at the Siege of Vienna in 1683.

OPPOSITE:
Sandwiches and quiche Lorraine in a Montmartre shop window, Place du Tertre

Quiche Lorraine is another type of food that may be less archetypally French than it appears. The word 'quiche' derives from the German 'kuchen', meaning cake, and the French version of quiche Lorraine reworks a traditional German dish.

RIGHT:
French cheese on display in a Paris supermarket

Most French supermarkets stock a wide range of cheeses, including many different types of each variety. It's not unusual to find shelves full of Camembert or Brie, for instance.

PREVIOUS PAGES:
Display of cheeses in a Paris shop window
More than fifty types of French cheese are designated under European law as having protected geographical status, meaning that they must be made within a certain region to be sold under that name. They include Gruyère, Pont-l'Évêque, and two types of Brie.

LEFT:
Edible land snails on sale at a market
Snails ('escargot' in French) are a popular French delicacy, usually cooked with garlic and parsley butter and served in their shells.

LEFT TOP:

Shellfish for sale at a market
Fresh seafood, including oysters, shrimp and whelks, can easily be bought in Paris, at the city's many fishmongers, or at its open-air markets, such as Marché Président-Wilson and Marché Bourse.

LEFT BOTTOM:

Fishmonger's stall
Paris's recently refurbished shopping centre, Forum des Halles, stands on the site of a former fresh food market demolished in the 1960s after eight centuries of existence. Farmers, fishmongers and butchers would all sell their wares there.

RIGHT:

Butcher's shop in Marché Beauvau, Place d'Aligre
Marché Beauvau, the indoor market at Place d'Aligre, opens six days a week in the mornings and late afternoons. Its three halls include a coffee shop, several butchers, a cheese shop and even a vegetarian butcher, La Boucherie Végétarienne!

ICI VIANDE DE CHEVAL

SPÉCIALITÉS

MEILLEURS COMMERCES DE BOUCHE PARIS

2009

OPPOSITE:
Butcher's shop at night
One of the more legendary
Paris butchers was Jean
l'écorcheur (literally, 'John
the skinner'), who was said
to have a sideline committing
murders for the royal family
in the 16th century. After he
too was killed on their orders,
he supposedly rose from the
grave and haunted the Louvre
for centuries, foretelling
several royal deaths.

RIGHT:
Paris delicatessen
Delicatessens are a common
sight on the streets of Paris.
One of the city's most
famous, Jo Goldenberg's,
stood in the Jewish quarter
of La Marais until 2008;
the clothing store that now
occupies the premises has
kept the delicatessen's name
and façade.

ABOVE:

À la mère de famille, Montmartre
Founded in 1761, À la mère de famille is the oldest sweetshop in
Paris; it also sells wine and ice cream. Though it now has several
satellite stores across the city, the original store, pictured here,
stands at the crossroads of rue du Faubourg Montmartre, rue
Cadet, rue de Provence and rue Richer.

RIGHT:

Vins et Terroirs restaurant, rue Saint-André-des-Arts
The traditional French restaurant Vins et Terroirs stands on the
historic Paris street rue Saint-André-des-Arts. This dates back
to the end of the 13th century at least, since it is mentioned in
the 554-verse poem of 1280–1300, *Le Dit des rues de Paris*, by
Guillot of Paris.

PLATEAU X DE COQUILLAGES

Plateau 2 pers   90 euros
...rteau, 1 homard 12 huîtres 6 Palourdes, 6 crevettes
2 Bulots, 6 moules, 4 lang., 2 clams)

Plateau 2 pers   55 euros
(1 tourteau, 12 huîtres, 4 crevettes, 8 Bulots, 8 moules, 2 pal.)

SPÉCIAL CRUSTACÉS
Plateau 1 pers   33 euros
6 crevettes, 12 Bulots, 1/2 tourteau, 4 langoustines)

Plateau 1 pers   3? euros
...6 Bulots, 4 crevettes,

OPPOSITE:

Chalked menu board outside a restaurant

Many French restaurants display their menus on blackboards outside the restaurant itself, to attract passers-by. This particular menu offers a variety of shellfish options ('plateaux de coquillages'), including oysters ('huîtres') and lobster ('homard').

RIGHT:

Paris street café

A sign at this retro Paris street café offers Absinthe de Pontarlier alongside Vermouth, beer and lemonade. Before absinthe was banned in 1915 due to its psychoactive properties, Pontarlier was one of its main producers; since the repeal of the ban in 2009, its distilleries are once again producing the notorious green liquor.

Landmarks, Ancient and Modern

From the top of the Eiffel Tower, 324m (1000ft) high, to the extensive catacombs beneath its streets, Paris is full of striking landmarks that offer glimpses into the city's often turbulent history. Many have changed either their name or their function over the course of the past millennium. Both the Louvre and the Conciergerie were once royal palaces, and the magnificent Musée d'Orsay started out as a railway station. La Place de la Revolution, which saw the execution of King Louis XVI and Queen Marie Antoinette in 1793, is now the more peaceful-sounding La Place de la Concorde.

The city's sheer variety is reflected in its buildings: the striking modern architecture of the Pompidou Centre stands just a few streets away from one of the city's oldest houses: 51 rue Montmorency, built in 1407. Its many open public spaces – the parks and squares that are to be found across Paris – are equally diverse, from the ultra-modern Parc André Citroën in the west to Père Lachaise Cemetery in the east.

In this chapter, we'll take a tour of some of Paris's most outstanding sights – its museums, galleries, statues and sculptures – and learn more about its remarkable past. We'll travel from the skyscrapers of the 15th arrondissement to the historic heart of the city at Île de la Cité, and from the reading room at the national library to the celebration of consumption that is Galeries Lafayette, to uncover the secrets of this beautiful and historic city.

OPPOSITE:

Small Pyramid, Louvre Palace
The great glass and metal pyramid that serves as the main entrance to the Louvre Museum is flanked by three smaller pyramids, one of which is pictured here. Designed by architect I.M. Pei and completed in 1989, the modernist pyramids offer a striking contrast to the classical Renaissance style of the palace itself.

LEFT:
Main Hall, Louvre Palace
The Louvre, the world's largest and most popular art museum, has occupied the Louvre Palace since 1793. Originally the site of a fortress, the Louvre has also served as the Paris residence for French kings, and the home of the royal academies.

ABOVE:
West Façade, Church of Saint-Sulpice
Saint-Sulpice, the second-largest church in Paris, houses three murals by Eugène Delacroix and a large 18th-century organ, but is increasingly well known for its gnomon, a device for calculating the position of the sun and therefore the exact time. Its west façade, pictured here, was designed by Giovanni Servandoni.

RIGHT:
Écoute, **Place René Cassin**
Situated in front of the Church of Saint-Eustache, this giant sculpture of a stone head and cupped hand was created by French artist Henri de Miller in 1986. Made of sandstone, it weighs 63 tonnes (70 tons).

BELOW:

Maman, Jardin de Tuileries, Paris

Artist Louise Bourgeois was born in Paris in 1911. *Maman*, her massive sculpture of a spider, has travelled around the world since its creation in 1999, and spent 2007–08 in the Jardin de Tuileries.

RIGHT:

Bulls' heads, Lavirotte Building, Paris

Architect Jules Lavirotte won an award in 1901 for the elaborate art nouveau façade of this building on avenue Rapp, in the 7th arrondissement. Among the many sculptures to be found are these two bulls, supporting the central balcony.

OPPOSITE:

Le Stryge, Notre-Dame

Notre-Dame's striking chimeras – not to be confused with the gargoyles that carry rainwater away from the building – were added to the cathedral during Viollet-le-Duc's restoration in 1845. The best-known of these is Le Stryge, 'the vampire', pictured here gazing out over the city.

RIGHT:

Ceiling and interior, Notre-Dame

The foundations of Notre-Dame were laid in 1163, replacing an earlier cathedral on the same site, Saint Stephen's. Immortalized in Victor Hugo's 1831 novel, *Notre-Dame de Paris*, the cathedral suffered the destruction of many of its statues during the French Revolution.

From the west, Île de la Cité
The oldest part of Paris, Île de la Cité is home to several medieval buildings. The spire of Notre-Dame Cathedral can be seen at the top of this picture, while to the left is the Conciergerie, where Marie Antoinette was imprisoned before her execution.

LEFT:

**Vendôme Column,
Place Vendôme**

The statue of Napoleon at the top of the Vendôme Column is the third to have stood there; the original was melted down following the Bourbon restoration. The entire column was dismantled during the Paris Commune in 1871 but reassembled several years later.

ABOVE:

**Colonne de Juillet,
Place de la Bastille**

A winged figure of Liberty stands at the top of the Colonne de Juillet, built to commemorate the July Revolution of 1830. It stands in the Place de la Bastille, the site of the notorious Parisian prison, destroyed in 1789.

**Luxor Obelisk,
Place de la Concorde**
The ancient obelisk that
stands at the centre of the
Place de la Concorde arrived
in Paris in 1833, a gift from
Egypt's then ruler. Its twin
still stands at the entrance to
the Luxor Temple in the city
once known as Thebes.

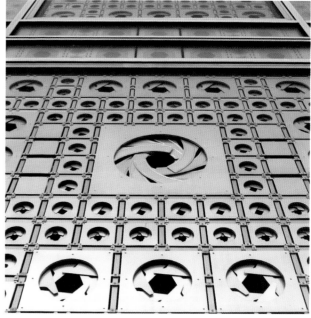

OPPOSITE:

Looking down at the Parc du Champ-de-Mars from the Eiffel Tower

The vast green space of the Champ-de-Mars stretches from the Eiffel Tower to the École Militaire, which formerly used it as a training ground.

LEFT:

View of the Eiffel Tower from below

Built to mark the tenth Exposition Universelle in 1889, the Eiffel Tower was originally only intended to last for twenty years. Its wrought-iron structure weighs around 9000 tonnes (10,000 tons).

ABOVE:

Looking up at the modern windows of the Institut du Monde Arabe

Designed by Jean Nouvel and inspired by screens from Moorish palaces, the dilating windows of the Institut du Monde Arabe expand or contract to regulate how much sunlight enters the building.

View of the Eiffel Tower and Front-de-Seine, Paris
The Front-de-Seine area in the 15th arrondissement is home to
many skyscrapers, including the Tour Crystal, Tour Totem and
the Tour de Mars. All are dwarfed by the 324m (1000 ft) high
Eiffel Tower, however.

Skyscrapers at night, La Défense
Named after the statue *La Défense de Paris*, which
commemorates the soldiers who defended Paris during the
Franco–Prussian war of 1870–71, La Défense is the largest
purpose-built business district in Europe.

Reflection in La Géode, Parc de la Villette
Situated in the Parc de la Villette, the geodesic steel dome La
Géode was designed by architect Adrien Fainsilber. At 36m
(118ft) in diameter, it houses an omnimax cinema with a
hemispheral screen of 1000 sq m (10,000 sq ft).

RIGHT AND BELOW:

Exterior, the Pompidou Centre
Opened in 1977, the Pompidou Centre houses a notable
collection of modern art. Its remarkable design, created by
architects Richard Rogers and Renzo Piano, places the entirety
of the centre's infrastructure, from pipes and escalators to
supporting structures, on the outside of the building.

Palais de Chaillot, Place du Trocadéro
Built for the 1937 Exposition Internationale, the Palais de Chaillot stands at the top of a hill in the Place du Trocadéro. It houses museums on ethnology, architecture and the navy, and offers an excellent view of the Eiffel Tower.

OPPOSITE:
Waterfall, Parc de Bercy,
Formerly the site of 19th-century wine warehouses, the fourteen-acre Parc de Bercy opened in 1994. Its three gardens are named La Grande Prairie ('the great prairie'), Les Parterres ('the formal gardens'), and Jardin Romantique ('the romantic garden').

RIGHT:
The grand staircase, the Palais Garnier
Opened in 1875, the Palais Garnier is known worldwide as the setting for Gaston Leroux's novel *The Phantom of the Opera*, and its many subsequent adaptations. Its grand staircase, pictured here, is made of white marble, with a balustrade of red and green marble.

LEFT:

Exterior, the Conciergerie
A royal palace until Charles V moved his court to the Louvre in 1358, the Conciergerie has been a prison and palace of justice since the late 14th century. It takes its name from the Concierge, an official appointed by the king to run the palace.

RIGHT:

Square Keep, Château de Vincennes
Like the Conciergerie, the Château de Vincennes has served at different times as both royal residence and prison; the Marquis de Sade was held here before being transferred to the Bastille in 1784.

Notre-Dame Cathedral from beneath Pont Saint-Michel, Île de la Cité
The oldest part of the city, the Île de la Cité is connected to the rest of Paris by several bridges crossing the Seine. The view here is from beneath Pont Saint-Michel; there has been a bridge at this place for more than 600 years; but this one dates from 1857.

Main Hall, the Musée d'Orsay
Housed in a former railway station built for the Exposition Universelle of 1900, the Musée d'Orsay opened in 1986 to exhibit art from the period 1848 to 1918. Its collection of impressionist and post-impressionist works is unrivalled.

ABOVE AND RIGHT:
Place des Vosges, Le Marais
One of the oldest squares in Paris, Place des Vosges was commissioned in 1605 by King Henry IV. Today, the mansions that surround it house restaurants, galleries and museums, including one dedicated to Victor Hugo, author of *Les Misérables*, who lived here from 1832 to 1848.

Sunset, le Jardin des Tuileries

Taking its name from the tile factories that formerly stood on the site, the Jardin des Tuileries once formed the gardens of the magnificent Palais des Tuileries, commissioned by Catherine de Medici in 1564. Set alight by the Paris Communards in 1871, the palace was completely gutted; more than a decade later, it was finally demolished, and its gardens extended.

OPPOSITE:
Dancing Fountains, Parc André Citroën
Named after the founder of the Citroën automobile company, whose factory occupied the site for much of the 20th century, the Parc André Citroën opened in 1992. A tethered helium balloon, the Ballon Generali, offers visitors the chance to view the city from a height of 150m (500ft).

RIGHT:
Fontaine des Fleurs, Place de la Concorde
Originally known as Place Louis XV, this square was renamed Place de la Revolution during the French Revolution, when it served as a site of execution; both King Louis XVI and his wife Marie Antoinette were guillotined here. It gained its current title in 1795, and its two fountains were added in the 19th century.

LEFT:
Sunset, Arc de Triomphe
Built between 1806 and 1836, the Arc de Triomphe stands at the centre of Place Charles de Gaulle, and honours those who fought for France.

OPPOSITE TOP LEFT:
Ceiling, Arc de Triomphe
The Arc de Triomphe features sculptures, friezes and bas-reliefs from a multitude of artists, including James Pradier, Antoine Étex and François Rude. Pictured here are the 21 roses on the underside of the arch.

OPPOSITE TOP RIGHT:
Staircase, Arc de Triomphe,
To reach the viewing platform at the Arc de Triomphe, 50m (150 ft) above the ground, a visitor must climb 234 steps.

OPPOSITE BOTTOM:
View of the Champs-Élysées from the Arc de Triomphe
The Arc de Triomphe offers magnificent vistas over the entire city. In the centre of this picture we can see the Champs-Élysées; at the top right, the 210m (700ft) high Tour Montparnasse.

OPPOSITE:
Dome, Galeries Lafayette

Founded by cousins Théophile Bader and Alphonse Kahn in
1893, Galeries Lafayette began life as a haberdashery within
a larger store, but soon expanded to encompass five entire
buildings. Its trademark dome, pictured here, is adorned
by neo-Byzantine style stained glass windows designed by
Jacques Grüber.

ABOVE:
Reading room, Bibliothèque Nationale de France

The national library of France has its origins in the private
collection of King Charles V, but grew following its establishment
in 1537 as France's legal deposit library, entitled to receive a
copy of any printed book for sale in the country. Though this
status was suspended during the French Revolution, the library
expanded through the acquisition of collections confiscated from
elsewhere. It now spans several different sites; the picture shows
the reading room at the Richelieu site, opened in 1868.

LEFT:

Ceiling of the Grand Foyer, the Palais Garnier
The paintings on the ceiling of the massive Grand Foyer at the Palais Garnier depict moments in the history of music. They were painted by Paul-Jacques-Aimé Baudry, who prepared for this mammoth task, which took ten years to complete, by travelling to Rome to study the Sistine Chapel ceiling.

OPPOSITE:

Place du Tertre, Montmartre
Once at the heart of the Paris art scene, Montmartre was home to artists including Picasso, Georges Braque and Maurice Utrillo. Today, there is a ten-year waiting list to occupy one of the around 150 1 sq m (10 sq ft) spaces allotted to artists in the Place du Tertre, not far from Sacré-Cœur.

OPPOSITE:

Sacré-Cœur, Montmartre
The Basilica of Sacré-Cœur stands at the top of the city's highest point, the Butte Montmartre, a place of worship since ancient Gaulish times. It is seen here through the face of the clock at the top of the Musée d'Orsay.

LEFT:

Clock, Conciergerie
The clock tower at the Conciergerie dates from the 14th century, and the clock itself from the 16th. The figures to either side of the clock face represent Justice and Law, and were created by Germain Pilon.

BELOW:

Gallery of Evolution, National Museum of Natural History
Formally founded in 1793, but dating back to the royal garden of medicinal plants established by King Louis XIII in 1635, the National Museum of Natural History includes across its many sites laboratories, exhibition galleries and a zoo.

Père Lachaise Cemetery
Opened in 1804, Père Lachaise has become the largest cemetery in Paris. It is visited by more than 3.5 million people each year, making it the most visited cemetery in the world. Its famous residents include writers Honoré de Balzac, Molière, Georges Perec, Marcel Proust and Oscar Wilde; singers Edith Piaf and Jim Morrison; and the painters Géricault, Ingres, Pissarro and Seurat. The cemetery also features several striking memorials to those residents of Paris murdered in the concentration camps of World War II.

**The tomb of Oscar Wilde,
Père Lachaise Cemetery,**
Carved and chiselled from
an 18-tonne (20-ton) block
of stone by sculptor Jacob
Epstein, the tomb of Oscar
Wilde features a vast winged
figure of a sphinx, or 'demon-
angel'; since 2011, it has been
shielded by a glass screen to
protect it from graffiti.

ABOVE:

Interior, the Panthéon
Built originally as a church in the reign of King Louis XV, the Panthéon was converted into a mausoleum during the French Revolution. It now houses the remains of Voltaire, Rousseau, Hugo and Zola.

RIGHT:

Catacombs, Montparnasse
Formerly underground stone quarries, the catacombs of Paris now hold the bones of more than six million people; their remains were removed from the city's overflowing and infectious cemeteries in the late 18th century.

The City of Light

Paris comes into its own after dark, when artificial light casts a magical orange glow over the city. Though it gained its reputation as the city of light from its role in the Enlightenment, when writers and philosophers such as Rousseau and Voltaire argued for reason and thought over dogma and faith, Paris has long since become as well known for its actual lights as for its thinkers. The gas street lamps introduced in 1828 along the Champs-Élysées were the first in Europe; and the electric lighting that spread across the city from the late 1870s was another innovation.

The city's nightlife has been famous since the heyday of the Moulin Rouge at the turn of the 20th century, when dancers of doubtful reputation entertained audiences in Montmartre with the can-can and other extravagant performances. Today, many of Paris's bars and restaurants stay open long after midnight, even on weekdays; its clubs stay open even later. Most of the city's museums open late one evening a week, and the Eiffel Tower – which stays open until around midnight to offer the best view of the city at night – casts its own light over Paris with its hourly light show. From La Grande Arche de la Défense and Notre-Dame on the Île de la Cité to neon signs and inviting lights on the plethora of bars, restaurant and cafés that lines the streets, many of the city's most striking sights are illuminated at night, and well worth a visit.

OPPOSITE:
Electric street lighting on Pont Alexandre III
Paris's distinctive street lighting helps the city maintain its unique character at night. Some of its most ornate lamp posts can be seen here on the Pont Alexandre III, where candelabra in an art nouveau style hold multiple lamps.

ABOVE:

Streetlight illuminated at night, Place de l'Hôtel de Ville
Electric street lighting first came to Paris in May 1878, to
celebrate the opening of the Exposition Universelle. Those
early electric lights, invented by Paris-based Russian Pavel
Nikolayevich Yablochkov, were known as 'Yablochkov candles'.

RIGHT:

Entrance to the Metro, Montmartre
The Paris Metro remains one of the most popular ways of
returning home after a night out in the city. The last trains –
known as 'balais' ('brooms'), because they sweep up the final
passengers – arrive at their terminus at around 1.15 a.m. each
night, except on Fridays, Saturdays and days before public
holidays, when the network stays open an hour later.

OPPOSITE:

**The Japan Bridge,
La Défense**

Built in 1993, the Japan Bridge
provides a pedestrian walkway
high above a seven-lane
highway between two office
buildings – Kupka and Le Tour
Pacifique – in the business
district of La Défense.

RIGHT:

**Walking home after work in
the business districts of Paris**

Though the French
government introduced a
35-hour work week in 2000,
with the aim of reducing
unemployment and improving
workers' quality of life,
many employees still work
longer hours.

LEFT:

The Eiffel Tower and Pont Neuf

Open until around midnight every night, the Eiffel Tower offers a wonderful opportunity to see Paris live up to its reputation as the 'city of light'. Though the name may have derived originally from the city's role in the Enlightenment, it was reinforced by its early adoption of streetlighting.

ABOVE:

The Champs-Élysées, from L'Arc de Triomphe

The headlights and taillights from ten lanes of traffic help light up the Champs-Élysées, one of Paris's most famous roads, each evening. Since 2016 the avenue has been closed to vehicles on the first Sunday of every month in a bid to cut pollution.

BELOW:

Exterior, La Cité de la Mode et du Design

Designed by architects Jakob + Macfarlane, the bright green glasswork of La Cité de la Mode et du Design ('the city of fashion and design') is at its most striking at night. Built on the site of the former docks, it combines exhibition spaces with a club and restaurant.

RIGHT:

Paris at dusk

Before electrical street lighting became the norm in Paris, the city used other means of lighting its streets at night. An edict in 1524 stated that all Parisian houses that faced the street must have lights in their windows at night; oil lanterns began to be installed in the 17th century.

OPPOSITE:

Parc de la Villette

Open until 1 a.m. each night, the Parc de la Villette includes a concert hall and museum alongside its playgrounds, ponds and fountains. Built on the site of historic abattoirs, it also hosts an open-air film festival each summer.

OPPOSITE:
Clock face at the Musée d'Orsay
Most Paris museums open late one night a week, most commonly on Thursday evenings, when the Musée d'Orsay (whose famous clock is pictured) doesn't close until 9.45 p.m., making its first-floor restaurant an enviable location for dinner.

ABOVE:
La Grande Roue, la Place de la Concorde
The Grand Roue Ferris Wheel has been a regular visitor to la Place de la Concorde since 1993, providing a striking contrast to the ancient Luxor Obelisk. However, it will leave the square in 2018 after councillors voted not to renew its licence.

LEFT:

The Moulin Rouge, Montmartre

The Moulin Rouge opened in 1889, taking its name from the red windmill ('moulin rouge') on its roof. Its transgressive cabaret embodied the decadence of fin-de-siècle Paris, and attracted the attention of artists such as Toulouse-Lautrec. Though the original building burned down in 1915, it was rebuilt, and reopened in 1921.

RIGHT:

The Eiffel Tower at night

On the hour, between sunset and 1 a.m. each night, the usual yellow lighting (pictured) at the Eiffel Tower is turned off for five minutes and a light show takes place: 20,000 tiny lights flash on and off on the tower itself while searchlights sweep across the city.

Exterior, Petit Palais
Opened in 1900 for that year's
Exposition Universelle, the
Petit Palais has been a museum
since 1902, and houses works
by Paul Cézanne, Gustave
Courbet, Eugène Delacroix,
Paul Gauguin and Claude
Monet. Its temporary
exhibitions open until 9 p.m.
on Friday evenings.

**View of the Arc de
Triomphe from the
Champs-Élysées**
In 1923, an eternal flame
was instituted at the Arc de
Triomphe, which serves as a
memorial to those who fought
for France. Each evening,
at 6:30 p.m., the flame is
rekindled by representatives
of one of France's many
veterans' organizations,
and wreaths decorated with
red, white and blue are laid
alongside it.

RIGHT:

La Grande Arche de la Défense, and the modern buildings of La Défense district

Originally built from concrete, glass and Italian marble (which was replaced with granite during its recent refurbishment), and resembling a hollowed cube, La Grande Arche de la Défense opened on 14 July 1989, the 200th anniversary of the French Revolution. Its popular rooftop restaurant reopened in 2017.

OPPOSITE:

Musician at the Louvre

Buskers are a regular sight in Paris. Many ply their trade on the metro – you will often see entire bands passing from carriage to carriage – but others choose to perform at popular tourist locations. Here, a cellist plays outside the Louvre.

OPPOSITE:

The Montparnasse Tower dominates the Paris skyline
Most of the 59 floors of the 210m (689ft) high Montparnasse Tower are occupied by offices, but the 56th houses a restaurant, and the top floor holds an observation deck that is said to offer the best views of the city…because the controversial tower itself cannot be seen from there!

RIGHT:

Exterior, Hôtel de Ville
Though the Hôtel de Ville has been the home of the Paris City Council since 1357, the current building was burnt down by the Communards in 1871, leaving only its stone shell remaining. Reconstruction work rebuilt the hall within this shell and it reopened in 1892.

Neon signs proliferate in a popular tourist area
Though most Parisians tend not to have dinner until after 8:30 p.m., restaurants in popular areas often open from 7 p.m. to cater for tourists. In the city's busiest districts, many stay open until after midnight.

**The Eiffel Tower, from
La Passerelle Debilly**
Neither the Eiffel Tower nor
the Passerelle Debilly was
intended to be still standing
in the 21st century. Both
were built originally for the
Exposition Universelle that
used to take place regularly
in Paris – the Eiffel Tower
for the 1889 edition, and
the Passerelle Debilly for
the 1900 version – and each
was meant to be demolished
several years later. Both
proved too popular to be
removed, however, though the
footbridge was relocated a
short way along the river.

OPPOSITE:

**Sacré-Cœur and
the Eiffel Tower**

Construction work on Sacré-Cœur began in 1875, more than a decade before the Eiffel Tower was erected. The basilica was not consecrated until 1919, however, thirty years after the wrought-iron tower opened to the public. Building work had been completed in 1914, but consecration was delayed by the outbreak of World War I.

RIGHT:

**The streets of
Montmartre at dusk**

Montmartre may be full of tourists these days, but sometimes, in the right light, its 19th-century incarnation as the home of painters including Degas, Matisse, Renoir and Toulouse-Lautrec doesn't seem so far away.

LEFT:

Street cafés on the Île Saint-Louis

The small island of Île Saint-Louis, just to the east of the ancient Île de la Cité, is home to cafés, restaurants, shops and stalls, offering everything from ice cream and crêpes to endless varieties of cheese.

RIGHT:

Art nouveau metro sign in Place Saint-Michel

At the heart of Paris's Latin Quarter is Place Saint-Michel. Its signature fountain was constructed by Gabriel Davioud and features work from nine different sculptors. Its metro station, Saint-Michel, is on line 4.

LEFT:

Cour du Commerce Saint-André, Odéon
One of the few Parisian streets to have retained its original cobblestones, Cour du Commerce Saint-André opened in 1776. It was here that German engineer and piano-maker Tobias Schmidt developed the guillotine, which would serve as France's chosen form of execution until 1977.

OPPOSITE:

Brasserie, early evening
Paris's popular brasseries first appeared in the 1870s after France lost the Franco–Prussian war and with it the province of Alsace. Many of the region's inhabitants fled to Paris, where they founded places to eat and drink beer.

RUE DES GRANDS DEGRES

LES GOURMANDS DE NOTRE DAME

BAR BRASSERIE

SERVICE NON STOP

CAFE

RESTAU... ATELI...

Café au Comptoir:
0.90
Sandwiches
sur place: 4
ou à emporter: 3.50
Planche de Charcuteries,
Planche de Fromages
ou Mixte: 14.00

Happy Hour
15h - 19h
sur
Bières Pression
25cl: 2.00
50cl: 4.00
Cocktails: 7
et ça continue à partir de 22h

Dining outside in Montmartre
Montmartre's picturesque rue Gabrielle was once home to Pablo Picasso, and now combines apartment blocks with bars, restaurants and shops. Its eastern end leads to the steps up to Sacré-Cœur.

OPPOSITE:
The Café de Paris on the Left Bank
Paris's Left Bank, on the southern side of the river Seine, has long been famed as the home of artists, writers and philosophers, attracting visitors including Gertrude Stein, Ernest Hemingway and F. Scott Fitzgerald. It remains a popular area for socializing.

LEFT TOP:
Café de Flore, Saint-Germain-des-Prés
One of Paris's oldest cafés, Café de Flore was a popular meeting place for many of France's greatest 20th-century writers. Jean-Paul Sartre, Simon de Beauvoir and Albert Camus often came here, as did Georges Bataille and Raymond Queneau.

LEFT BOTTOM:
Quai de Jemmapes, on the Canal Saint-Martin
The bars around the Canal Saint-Martin have in recent years become an increasingly popular place to spend long summer evenings, now that the docks that once dominated the area have been transformed into studios and student halls of residence.

LEFT TOP:

Le Consulat, Montmartre

The restaurant Le Consulat stands on the corner between rue Norvins and rue Saint-Rustique in Montmartre. A sign on its wall states that it was once the meeting place for painters including Picasso, Van Gogh, Monet and Toulouse-Lautrec.

LEFT BOTTOM:

Winter evening at Au Relais, Montmartre

The tables outside Paris restaurants remain popular even on cold winter evenings. Many, like La Relais, stay open until 2 a.m. and then reopen at 8 a.m. the next morning to cater for those on their way to or from work.

RIGHT:

Paris noir: cobblestones at night

The streets of Paris have been a popular setting for crime fiction ever since Edgar Allan Poe's short story, 'The Murders in the Rue Morgue', back in 1841. Georges Simenon's Parisian detective Maigret appeared in more than 70 novels and 28 short stories between 1931 and 1972.

OPPOSITE:

A row of bicycles for rent, the Latin Quarter

Paris's Vélib' bicycle-rental service offers an alternative way of getting home after a night out. A ride of under half an hour costs a maximum of 1 Euro (around 88p or $1.20), and there are bike stations across the city.

ABOVE:

Locked bicycle, Paris street

Cycling has become increasingly popular in Paris over recent decades, and journeys by bike are expected to outnumber journeys by car by 2030. Some 2.5 million tourists rent a bike each year.

RIGHT:

Les Pipos wine bar, Place LaRue

Not far from the Sorbonne, the historic home of Parisian academia, and the Ministry of Education, Les Pipos stands alongside bookshops, restaurants and bars in Paris's Latin quarter.

Christmas lights on Boulevard Haussmann
Named after the architect whose programme of renovations transformed the city between 1853 and 1870, Boulevard Haussmann stretches between the 8th and 9th arrondissements of Paris. Novelist Marcel Proust lived here between 1906 and 1919; his cork-lined bedroom has been recreated and is now displayed at the Musée Carnavalet.

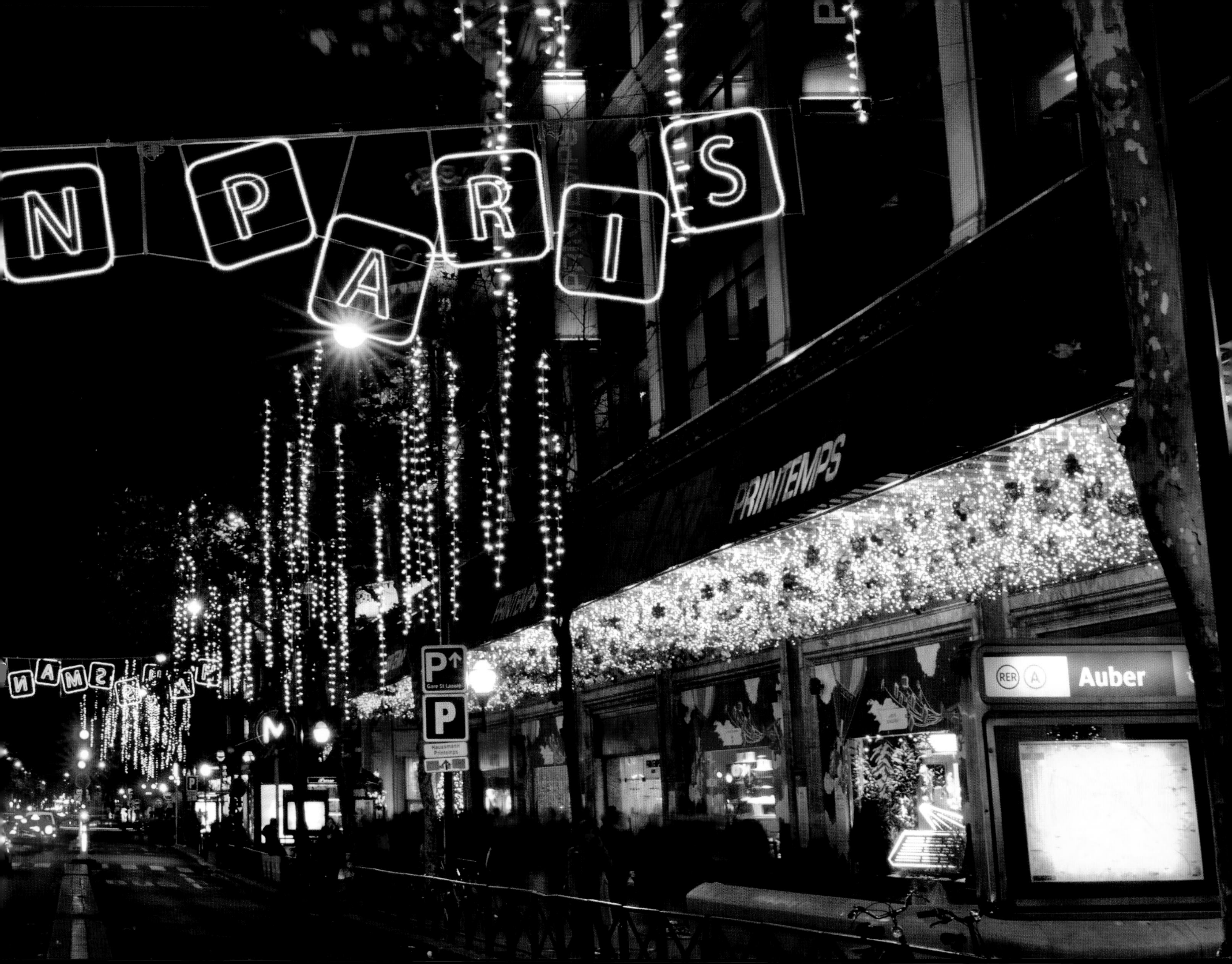
PARIS
PRINTEMPS
PRINTEMPS
RER A
Auber
P
P

LEFT:

Rooftops, Montmartre
The rooftops of Paris have provided inspiration for countless painters. Van Gogh's *View of the Roofs of Paris*, painted in the summer of 1886, can be found in Amsterdam's Van Gogh Museum, while Gustave Caillebotte's *Rooftops in the Snow* (1879) can be seen at the Musée d'Orsay.

OPPOSITE TOP:

Townhouses on the Quai des Orfèvres
Many of Paris's grand townhouses have been converted into single-storey apartments costing around 1m Euro (£990,000 or $1.2m) to buy. A multi-storey apartment on the Quai des Orfèvres, like those pictured here, can cost upwards of 10m Euro (£9m or $12m).

OPPOSITE BOTTOM:

Notre-Dame at night, from the Pont de la Tournelle
The bridge to the left of Notre-Dame, Pont de l'Archevêché ('the archbishop's bridge'), was built in 1828. It has recently become a popular place for lovers to place padlocks signifying their love.

The banks of the Seine in early evening
The paths along the banks of the river Seine bustle with activity, particularly during the long summer evenings. Since 2002, several sites along the river have been transformed each summer into temporary beaches through the addition of tons of sand, family activities, and even a swimming pool.

Beauty and Function: Transport in Paris

France's historic capital is a city traversed not only by trains and taxis but also by trams, bicycles, a funicular railway, and even – since 2017 – autonomous shuttles. As these photographs show, its transport network reflects the fact that this is a vibrant and bustling city that has grown and developed over more than a millennium, and is continuing to do so. Historic bridges now include dedicated cycle paths – appropriately enough for the city where the Tour de France finishes each year. Newly opened metro stations link the city's peripheries ever more closely with its ancient heart at the Île de la Cité. And its biggest railway station, Gare du Nord, is Europe's busiest, linking the city with Belgium, Germany, Great Britain and the Netherlands.

Everywhere, Paris combines functionality with beauty. The city's 300 metro stations are often as striking as they are useful, their beautiful entrances ranging from the gorgeous art nouveau designs of Hector Guimard to the futuristic lens design of Arte Charpentier's Saint-Lazare. The 37 bridges that cross the river Seine, joining the left bank to the right, are often equally outstanding, from the oldest, Pont Neuf, which dates from 1607, to the newest, the elegant Passerelle Simone-de-Beauvoir, which opened in 2006. Transport in Paris may be a necessity for the more than two million people who live in the city itself, and the ten million who live in the surrounding Île-de-France region, but it can also be a joy.

OPPOSITE:
Pedestrian entrance to Pont de Bir-Hakeim, rue de'Alboni
Built between 1903 and 1905, the Pont de Bir-Hakeim has two levels: an upper section that carries line 6 of the metro, and a lower section for pedestrians, cyclists and motor vehicles.

View of the Île de la Cité across Pont Neuf
The oldest bridge in Paris, Pont Neuf – whose name ironically means 'new bridge' – is also the city's most famous. Joining the historic Île de la Cité to the rest of the city, it was officially opened by King Henry IV in 1607.

LEFT:
Nymph, Pont Alexandre III
Nymphs look out across the river from each side of the Pont Alexandre III's single, 109m (350ft) arch. Created by Georges Récipon, the Nymphs of the Seine represent France, and the Nymphs of the Neva, Imperial Russia.

ABOVE:
Taxi
Taxis have been seen on the streets of Paris since the early 17th century, originally drawn by horses. Perhaps their finest hour came during World War I, when 600 Paris taxis were used to transport 6000 French soldiers to reinforce the troops at the Battle of the Marne.

**Metro train crossing
Pont de Bercy**
Built between 1863 and 1864
to replace an old toll bridge,
Pont de Bercy has twice been
widened: once, in 1904, to
support the metro, and then
again between 1989 and
1992 to allow for increased
road traffic.

LEFT:
The Seine glows with light, Pont Notre-Dame
A bridge has stood at this point since ancient times, but this version dates from 1919. One bridge, lined with sixty houses, collapsed in 1499; another, which became known as the 'Devil's bridge', was involved in more than 35 river traffic accidents in twenty years.

BELOW:
Art nouveau metro station canopy, Abbesses
Only two of Hector Guimard's original art nouveau Paris metro station canopies still exist; this one, situated at the Abbesses station in Montmartre, used to stand at Hôtel de Ville but was moved here in 1974.

RIGHT:
Art nouveau panelling, Porte Dauphine
The second remaining canopied Hector Guimard metro station is to be found at Porte Dauphine; it retains its original painted enamel panelling, adorned at the top with a dragonfly design.

RIGHT:

Art Nouveau ironwork, Abbesses

Guimard's metro station entrances are also notable for their ornate ironwork. Though his designs divided opinion on their first appearance in 1900, they underwent a renaissance in the 1960s, two decades after his death.

OPPOSITE:

Red metro sign

The familiar metro signs with white text cut out from a red background and a lamp attached to the top are known as 'candélabre Dervaux'. Designed by Adolphe Dervaux, they date originally from the 1920s.

Towards Montmartre sign, metro line 12
Line 12 of the Paris metro opened in 1910 as Line A, linking Montparnasse in the south with Montmartre in the north. Since then, it has been extended in both directions, and now stretches from Front Populaire in the north to Mairie d'Issy in the south.

OPPOSITE:
Line 11, Arts et Métiers metro station
This remarkable platform at the Arts et Métiers metro station was redesigned in 1994 by Belgian comic artist François Schuiten to celebrate the bicentenary of the nearby Conservatoire National des Arts et Métiers. Its copper panelling and portholes evoke the science fiction novels of Jules Verne.

RIGHT:
Metro station interior
First opened in 1900, the Paris metro system now comprises more than 300 stations across sixteen lines. It takes its name from the company that once ran most of the network: *La Compagnie du chemin de fer métropolitain de Paris.*

LEFT:
Staircase and platform, Cité metro station
The only metro station on the Île de la Cité, Cité station opened in 1910. Because of its depth, staircases lead from ground level first to a mezzanine ticketing level, and then down several further flights to the platform.

BELOW:
Train interior, metro
Several different types of trains are used on the Paris metro. The oldest, the MP59 model, dates from the 1960s; more recent models, such as the MP05, feature air-conditioning and automatic doors.

ABOVE:

Stalingrad metro station
Not all Paris metro stations are underground; more than twenty are in the open air. The glass-panelled walls and canopy of Stalingrad station stand more than 5m (16ft) above the street, allowing traffic to pass underneath.

RIGHT:

Bicycle lanes, Pont de Bercy
There are more than 700km (430 miles) of cycle lanes in Paris. Here we see two dedicated lanes on the Pont de Bercy, beneath the viaduct that carries trains from metro line 6.

View of the Eiffel Tower, Pont de Bir-Hakeim
Named after a World War II battle fought in Libya, this picturesque bridge is a popular site for photographers seeking views of the Eiffel Tower. It has also featured in several films, including *Zazie Dans le Métro*, *Last Tango in Paris* and *Inception*.

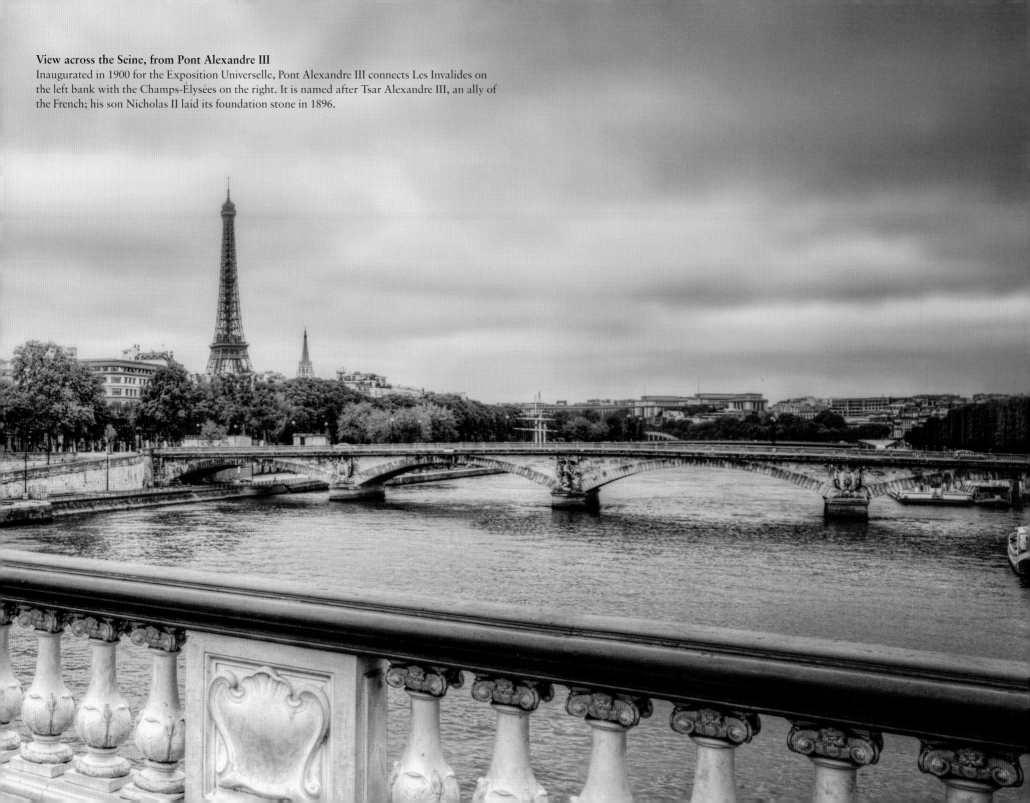

View across the Seine, from Pont Alexandre III
Inaugurated in 1900 for the Exposition Universelle, Pont Alexandre III connects Les Invalides on the left bank with the Champs-Élysées on the right. It is named after Tsar Alexandre III, an ally of the French; his son Nicholas II laid its foundation stone in 1896.

Grand Palais, from Pont Alexandre III
One of the city's most ornately decorated bridges, the Pont Alexandre III is guarded at each end by a pair of gilt bronze sculptures of winged horses. At its north end stands the Grand Palais, which opened in the same year (1900).